J

Notable Book—1972 c.38

221.95
S

Singer, Isaac Bashevis
The wicked city

Date Due   *4.50*

ADRIANCE MEMORIAL LIBRARY
POUGHKEEPSIE, N. Y.

Retells the Biblical story of Abraham's
wicked nephew Lot, of Lot's wife and daughters, of the bargain Abraham tried to make
with the Lord, and of the raging fire that
descended from the sky and destroyed the
city of Sodom.

The Wicked City

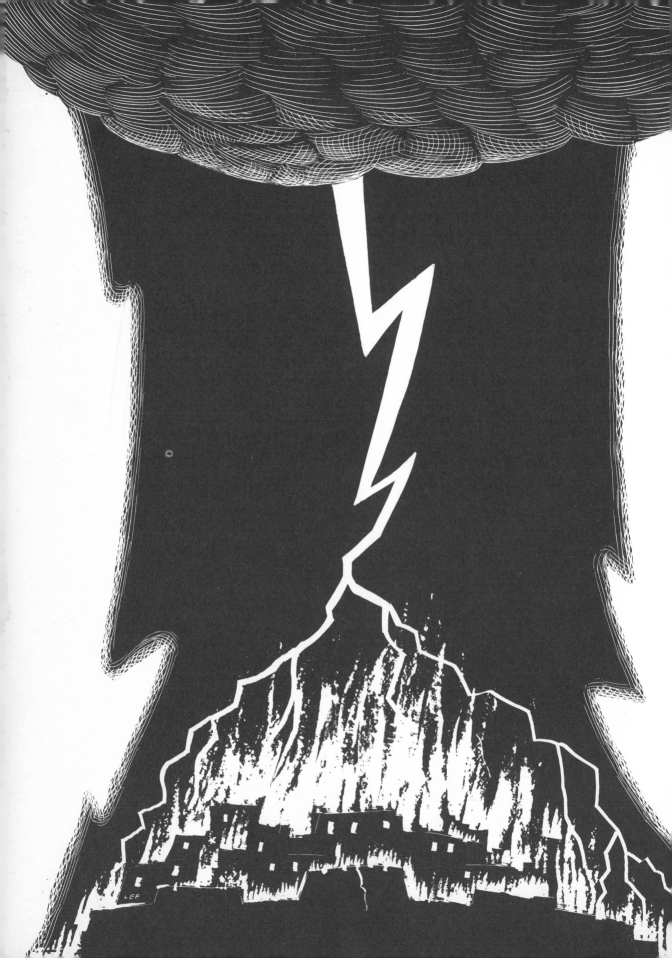

The Wicked City

ISAAC BASHEVIS SINGER

Pictures by Leonard Everett Fisher

Translated by the author and Elizabeth Shub

FARRAR, STRAUS AND GIROUX   NEW YORK

Text copyright © 1972 by Isaac Bashevis Singer
Pictures copyright © 1972 by Leonard Everett Fisher
All rights reserved
First printing, 1972
Library of Congress catalog card number 72-175144
ISBN 0-374-38426-6
Printed in the United States of America
Published simultaneously in Canada by Doubleday Canada Ltd., Toronto
Designed by Bobye List

The Wicked City

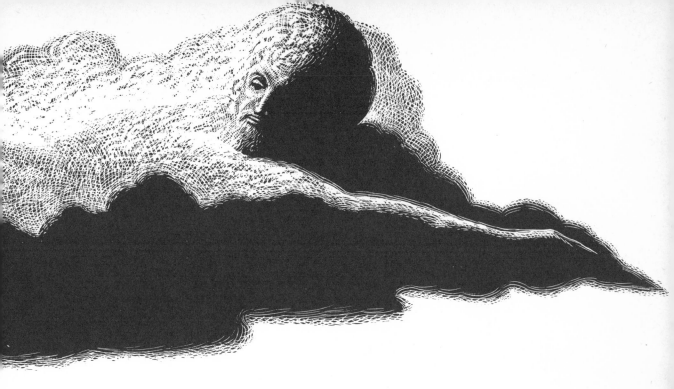

WHEN GOD commanded Abraham to leave
the land of Haran, his nephew Lot decided to
go with him. Lot was a lawyer in Haran, well
known for his defense of criminals. In such
matters he was very shrewd, though he had little
feeling for justice. He instructed his clients to lie,
hired false witnesses, and bribed the judges.

Lot had grown rich and powerful. He had a
large house, a pretty wife, and two lively
daughters, Bechirah and Tsirah. Nevertheless,
his wife was not content. She wanted more gold,
more pearls, and more slaves. She had heard
that Sodom was an immensely rich city where
there were many criminals who would need a
lawyer, and she persuaded Lot that they should
move there.

Abraham was a holy man, a servant of God, who knew nothing about the way his nephew conducted his affairs. God told Abraham to leave his country and he obeyed. When Lot suggested to him that they travel together in the direction of Canaan, which was near Sodom, his uncle readily agreed.

Before he left Haran, Lot sold his house, his cows, his oxen, his horses, his donkeys, and his camels. He and his family rode on Abraham's donkeys, ate his bread, and at night covered themselves with his animal hides.

Sarah, Abraham's wife, said to him, "Why does Lot use your belongings? He is not a poor man."

"He is my brother's son," Abraham replied. "Besides, we have no children and after our death he will inherit all we have. Why shouldn't he use now what will one day be his?"

When they approached the land of Canaan, God told Abraham that he was to settle there. But Lot said: "Uncle, I do not wish to remain a burden on you. I will go on to Sodom. I was told that there is a great need for lawyers there, and I surely will be able to earn my bread."

"Go and may God bless you," Abraham replied.

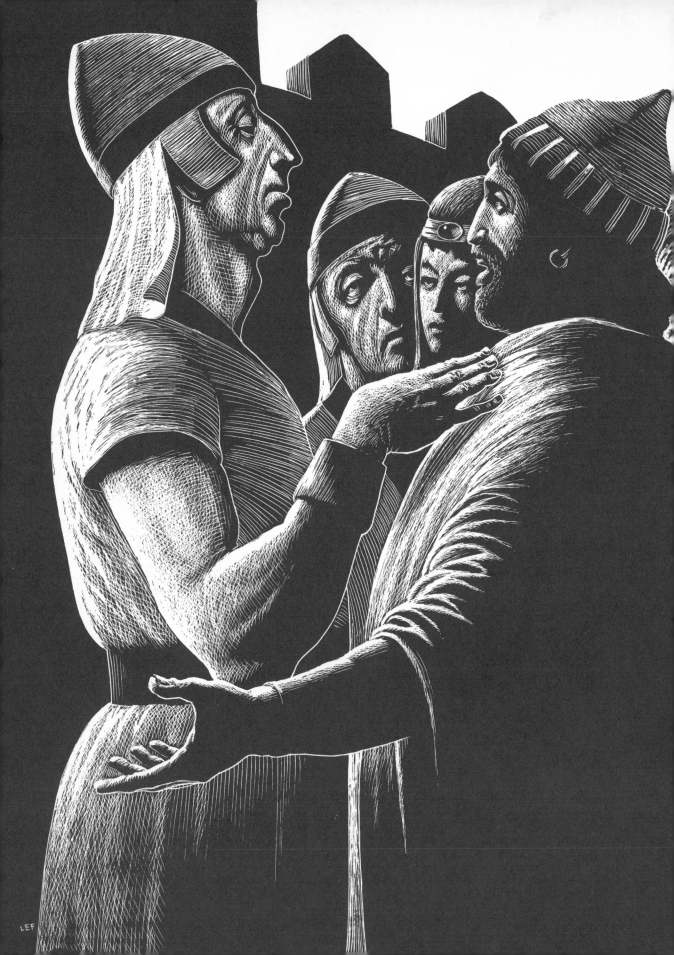

LOT LEFT for Sodom with his wife and daughters. When they arrived at the gates of the city, however, they were stopped. Strangers were banned from Sodom by law. The people were even forbidden to sell food to travelers. In those rare cases where a foreigner was allowed inside, he was usually killed during the night. Such was the custom of this sinful city.

Lot was about to turn back, but his wife addressed the gatekeepers: "My husband is a lawyer and a famous defender of criminals. In Haran there was a man who had murdered both his parents, but my husband got him off scot-free."

"How did he manage that?" asked one of the gatekeepers.

"He pointed out to the judge that the killer was an orphan and an orphan deserves mercy. The murderer was not only freed but inherited his parents' fortune as well and is now one of the richest men in Haran."

When the gatekeepers heard this story, they sent a messenger to the elders of Sodom. The elders were so impressed to hear of Lot's defense of the orphan that they not only decided to allow Lot to enter the city but invited him to remain and become a citizen of Sodom.

Lot quickly got used to Sodom and its customs. True, he spoke the local language with an accent, but otherwise he behaved like a born Sodomite.

His wife accustomed herself to Sodom's way of life even more readily. Once, when a beggar came to ask for bread, she replied, "I give only stale bread."

"I'm so hungry," the beggar said, "that even stale bread will satisfy me."

"But, alas, we baked today and the bread is still fresh. Come back in a few days. The bread will then be stale and I will give you some," Lot's wife said, although she knew very well that the beggar would die of hunger if he had to wait so long for food.

On another occasion, a peddler came to her and said: "I have two sacks of apples for which the usual price is a silver shekel per sack. But I am in need of cash, and so you may have both sacks of apples and I will only charge you for one. That gives you one sack free."

Lot's wife took one sack of apples but did not pay the peddler a penny.

"Why don't you pay me?" the peddler asked.

"I took the free sack," she replied. When he tried to argue, she set her dogs on him and he barely escaped with his life.

The neighbors who heard about these incidents were filled with admiration for Lot's wife. It wasn't long before she forbade her daughters to speak either Hebrew or Aramaic, the language of Haran. "In Sodom, behave like a Sodomite," she instructed them. She also told them never to mention their Great-uncle Abraham and their Great-aunt Sarah. "It is below our dignity as honorable citizens of Sodom to have an old fool in our family who believes in God and obeys his word," she said.

One day Lot's wife hired a drummer to walk the streets of Sodom and sing the praises of Lot. The drummer stood in the marketplace and called out: "My lord Lot in his wisdom is able to save from prison or death thieves, murderers, vandals, swindlers, and robbers. There has not been so great a defender of criminals as my employer since the days of the flood."

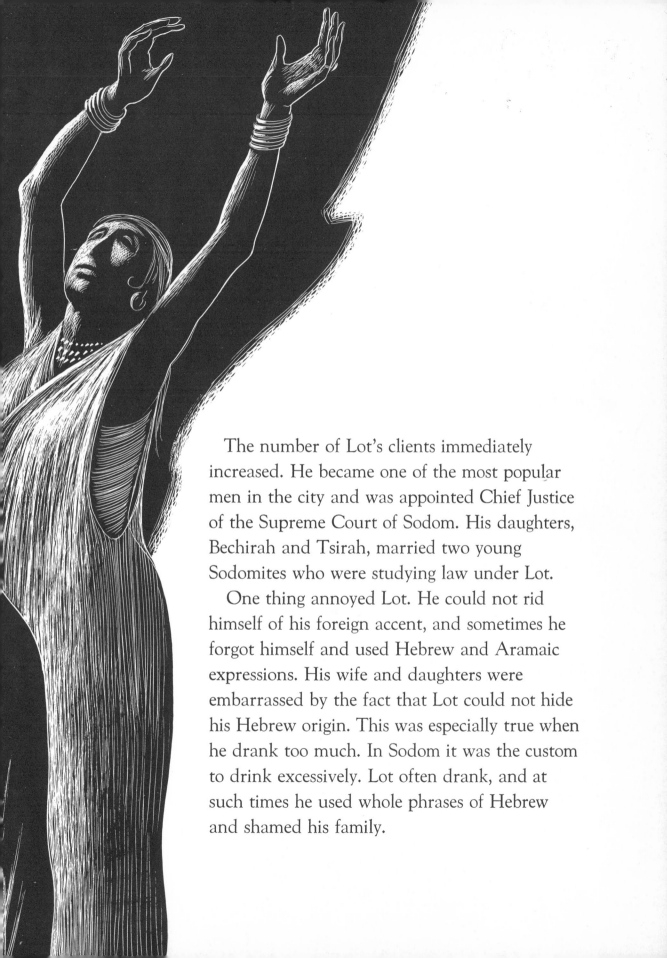

The number of Lot's clients immediately increased. He became one of the most popular men in the city and was appointed Chief Justice of the Supreme Court of Sodom. His daughters, Bechirah and Tsirah, married two young Sodomites who were studying law under Lot.

One thing annoyed Lot. He could not rid himself of his foreign accent, and sometimes he forgot himself and used Hebrew and Aramaic expressions. His wife and daughters were embarrassed by the fact that Lot could not hide his Hebrew origin. This was especially true when he drank too much. In Sodom it was the custom to drink excessively. Lot often drank, and at such times he used whole phrases of Hebrew and shamed his family.

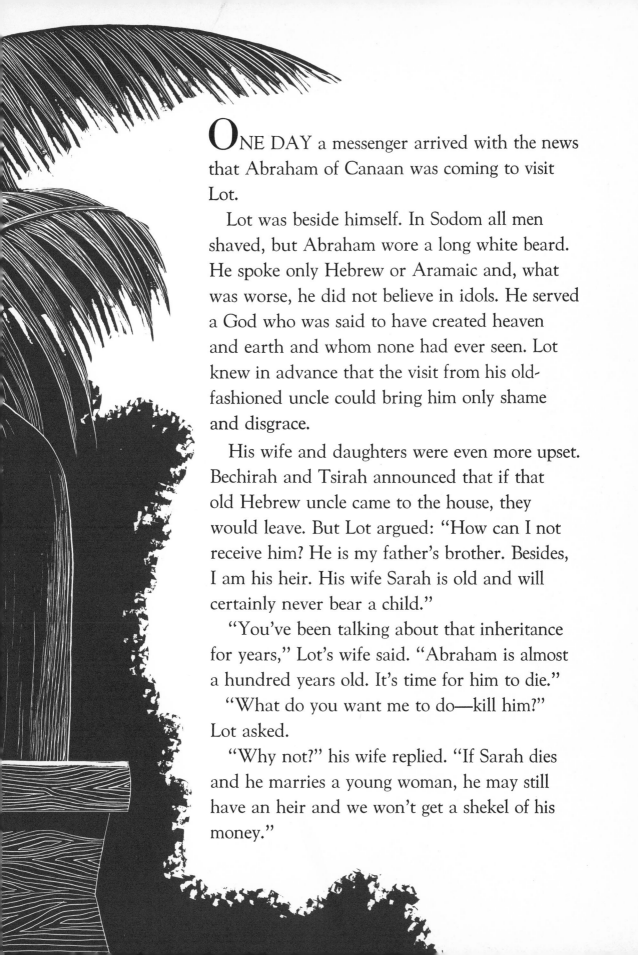

ONE DAY a messenger arrived with the news
that Abraham of Canaan was coming to visit
Lot.

Lot was beside himself. In Sodom all men
shaved, but Abraham wore a long white beard.
He spoke only Hebrew or Aramaic and, what
was worse, he did not believe in idols. He served
a God who was said to have created heaven
and earth and whom none had ever seen. Lot
knew in advance that the visit from his old-
fashioned uncle could bring him only shame
and disgrace.

His wife and daughters were even more upset.
Bechirah and Tsirah announced that if that
old Hebrew uncle came to the house, they
would leave. But Lot argued: "How can I not
receive him? He is my father's brother. Besides,
I am his heir. His wife Sarah is old and will
certainly never bear a child."

"You've been talking about that inheritance
for years," Lot's wife said. "Abraham is almost
a hundred years old. It's time for him to die."

"What do you want me to do—kill him?"
Lot asked.

"Why not?" his wife replied. "If Sarah dies
and he marries a young woman, he may still
have an heir and we won't get a shekel of his
money."

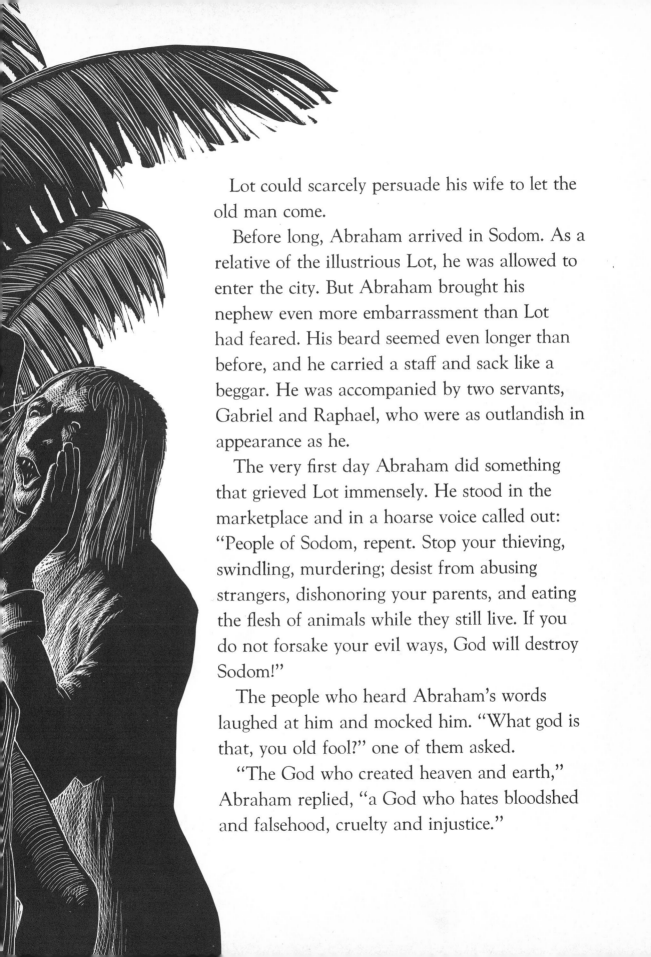

Lot could scarcely persuade his wife to let the old man come.

Before long, Abraham arrived in Sodom. As a relative of the illustrious Lot, he was allowed to enter the city. But Abraham brought his nephew even more embarrassment than Lot had feared. His beard seemed even longer than before, and he carried a staff and sack like a beggar. He was accompanied by two servants, Gabriel and Raphael, who were as outlandish in appearance as he.

The very first day Abraham did something that grieved Lot immensely. He stood in the marketplace and in a hoarse voice called out: "People of Sodom, repent. Stop your thieving, swindling, murdering; desist from abusing strangers, dishonoring your parents, and eating the flesh of animals while they still live. If you do not forsake your evil ways, God will destroy Sodom!"

The people who heard Abraham's words laughed at him and mocked him. "What god is that, you old fool?" one of them asked.

"The God who created heaven and earth," Abraham replied, "a God who hates bloodshed and falsehood, cruelty and injustice."

"Where is this god of yours? Of what is he made? Stone? Gold? Copper? Ivory?"

"Neither stone nor gold nor copper nor ivory. No one carved or cast him," Abraham answered. "He cannot be seen, but he has created the oceans, the mountains, the deserts, the people and animals. He is all merciful and provides for all that lives."

"Why did Lot allow his crazy uncle to come here?" one of the bystanders asked. Others pelted Abraham and his two companions with the dung of asses.

"This is what happens when one admits strangers," said another. "Sooner or later they bring other foreigners with them."

"He should be deported," cried a man in the crowd.

"No need to deport me," Abraham replied. "I do not want to stay. But I warn you for the last time. Repent!"

But no one showed any sign of repentance.

That evening in Lot's house Abraham repeated his warning: "Sodom will be destroyed." He said to Lot: "If you want to remain alive, rise at dawn, take your family and leave the city behind. Soon after the sunrise, there will be nothing left of Sodom but sulphur and ashes."

"The old man is insane," screamed Lot's wife, no longer able to contain her anger.

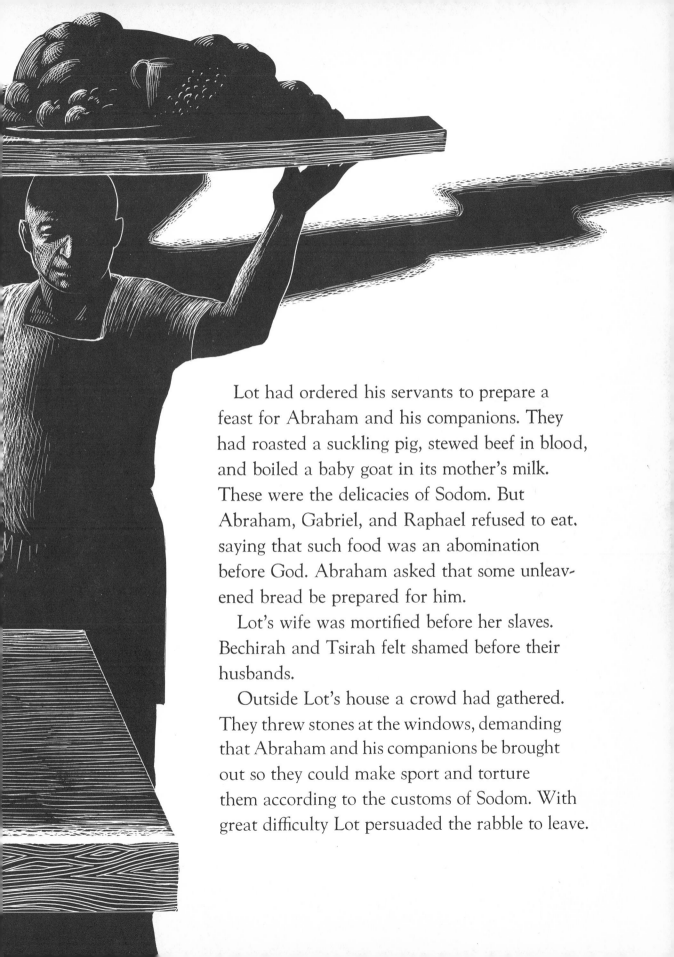

Lot had ordered his servants to prepare a feast for Abraham and his companions. They had roasted a suckling pig, stewed beef in blood, and boiled a baby goat in its mother's milk. These were the delicacies of Sodom. But Abraham, Gabriel, and Raphael refused to eat, saying that such food was an abomination before God. Abraham asked that some unleavened bread be prepared for him.

Lot's wife was mortified before her slaves. Bechirah and Tsirah felt shamed before their husbands.

Outside Lot's house a crowd had gathered. They threw stones at the windows, demanding that Abraham and his companions be brought out so they could make sport and torture them according to the customs of Sodom. With great difficulty Lot persuaded the rabble to leave.

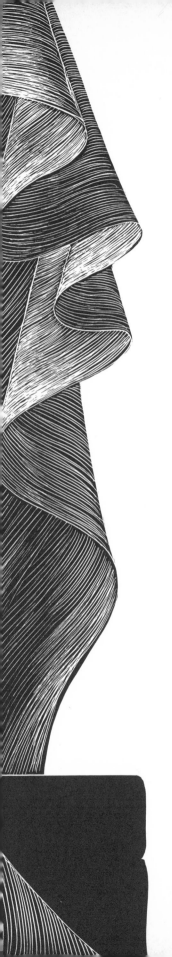

It was very late when Lot and his family went to bed, but Abraham and his companions did not retire. Lot, who could not sleep, overheard Abraham pleading with his God:

"Wilt thou destroy the just with the wicked? If there be fifty just men in the city, wilt thou also destroy and not spare the place for the fifty just that are therein? That be far from thee to do after this manner. . . . Shall not the judge of all the earth do right?

"What if there be five less than fifty just persons?

"What if there be forty found there?

"What if there be thirty found there?

"What if there be twenty found there?

"What if ten shall be found there?"

Lot's wife too had awakened. "The old man is certainly not in his right mind," she said to Lot. "If you do not get rid of him tomorrow, I will leave you and the court will make you turn over your entire fortune to me. You will have to pay me a thousand shekels a week or go to jail."

"I implore you to be quiet," Lot pleaded. "Is it my fault that I have a silly old uncle?"

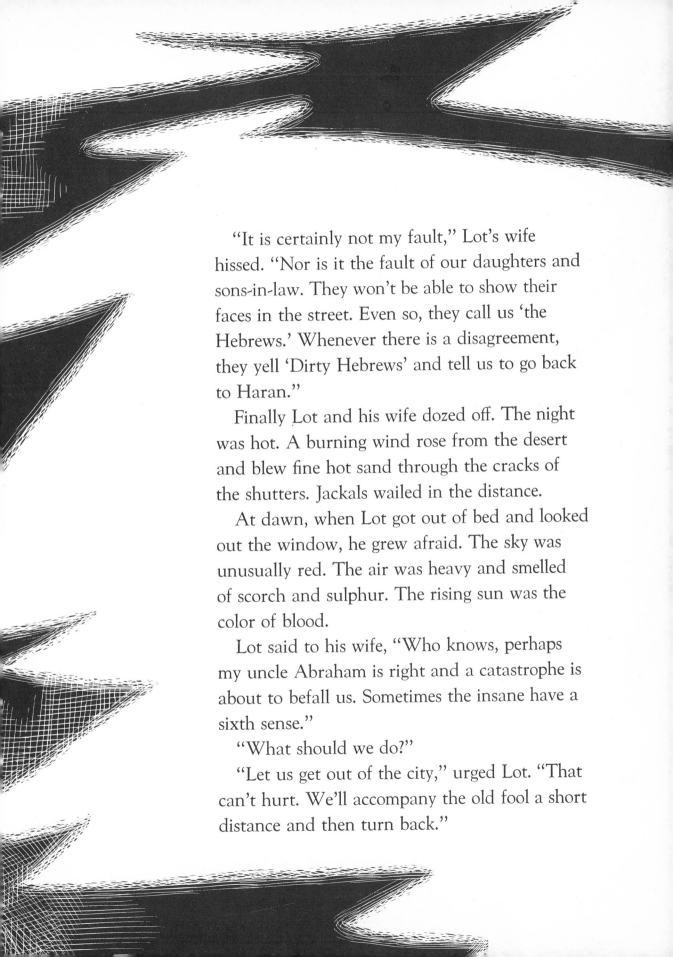

"It is certainly not my fault," Lot's wife
hissed. "Nor is it the fault of our daughters and
sons-in-law. They won't be able to show their
faces in the street. Even so, they call us 'the
Hebrews.' Whenever there is a disagreement,
they yell 'Dirty Hebrews' and tell us to go back
to Haran."

Finally Lot and his wife dozed off. The night
was hot. A burning wind rose from the desert
and blew fine hot sand through the cracks of
the shutters. Jackals wailed in the distance.

At dawn, when Lot got out of bed and looked
out the window, he grew afraid. The sky was
unusually red. The air was heavy and smelled
of scorch and sulphur. The rising sun was the
color of blood.

Lot said to his wife, "Who knows, perhaps
my uncle Abraham is right and a catastrophe is
about to befall us. Sometimes the insane have a
sixth sense."

"What should we do?"

"Let us get out of the city," urged Lot. "That
can't hurt. We'll accompany the old fool a short
distance and then turn back."

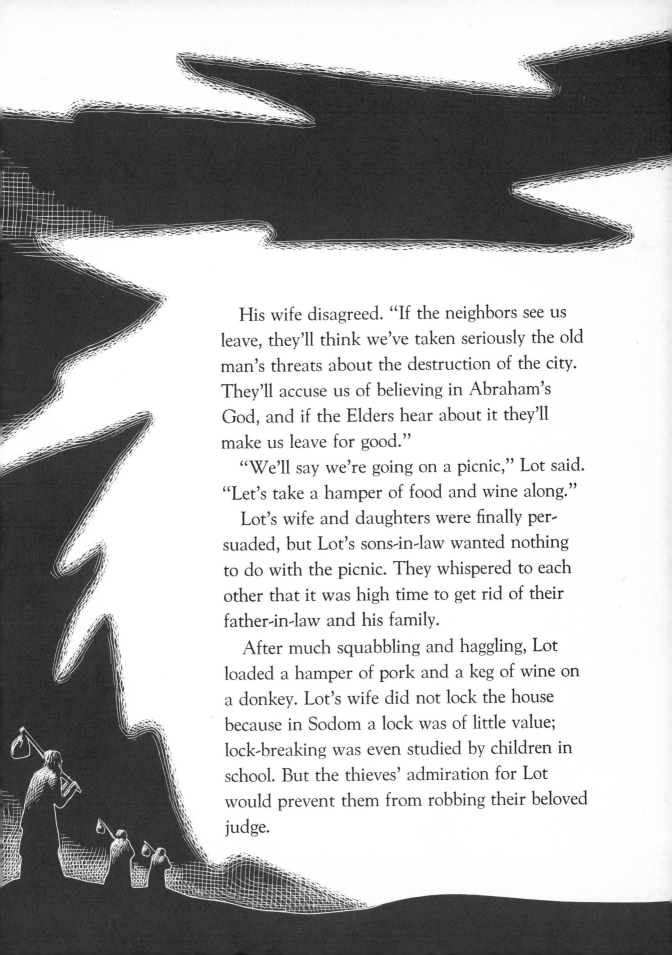

His wife disagreed. "If the neighbors see us leave, they'll think we've taken seriously the old man's threats about the destruction of the city. They'll accuse us of believing in Abraham's God, and if the Elders hear about it they'll make us leave for good."

"We'll say we're going on a picnic," Lot said. "Let's take a hamper of food and wine along."

Lot's wife and daughters were finally persuaded, but Lot's sons-in-law wanted nothing to do with the picnic. They whispered to each other that it was high time to get rid of their father-in-law and his family.

After much squabbling and haggling, Lot loaded a hamper of pork and a keg of wine on a donkey. Lot's wife did not lock the house because in Sodom a lock was of little value; lock-breaking was even studied by children in school. But the thieves' admiration for Lot would prevent them from robbing their beloved judge.

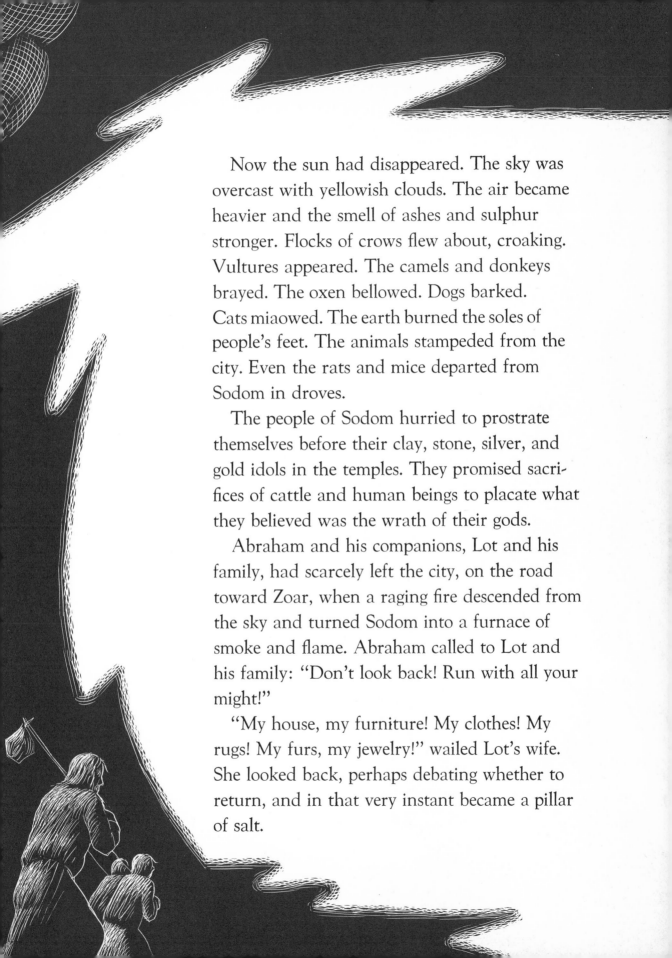

Now the sun had disappeared. The sky was overcast with yellowish clouds. The air became heavier and the smell of ashes and sulphur stronger. Flocks of crows flew about, croaking. Vultures appeared. The camels and donkeys brayed. The oxen bellowed. Dogs barked. Cats miaowed. The earth burned the soles of people's feet. The animals stampeded from the city. Even the rats and mice departed from Sodom in droves.

The people of Sodom hurried to prostrate themselves before their clay, stone, silver, and gold idols in the temples. They promised sacrifices of cattle and human beings to placate what they believed was the wrath of their gods.

Abraham and his companions, Lot and his family, had scarcely left the city, on the road toward Zoar, when a raging fire descended from the sky and turned Sodom into a furnace of smoke and flame. Abraham called to Lot and his family: "Don't look back! Run with all your might!"

"My house, my furniture! My clothes! My rugs! My furs, my jewelry!" wailed Lot's wife. She looked back, perhaps debating whether to return, and in that very instant became a pillar of salt.

"Woe, woe, see what has happened to our mother," Lot's daughters screamed. Lot tried to take his wife by the arm and when he saw that she did not move he put his hand to his mouth in fright. It tasted of salt. "Salt! My wife has turned into salt!" he wailed.

Abraham, however, urged them on, and only after they had covered a good distance did he permit them to stop and look back. What had been a teeming city only a short while before was now a mountain of smoldering ashes.

"Lot," Abraham said, "know you that my companions Gabriel and Raphael are angels. Now that you see the truth, repent and turn to God."

"What truth? I believe neither in God nor in angels," Lot said.

"But you see what has happened to Sodom," Abraham insisted.

"The volcano erupted. It has nothing to do with your God and his angels."

Turning to the angels, Abraham said, "He will remain as he is until he dies. Let us go on our way."

"Uncle Abraham," Lot said, "will you first give me part of my inheritance? You will soon die and I have no money left."

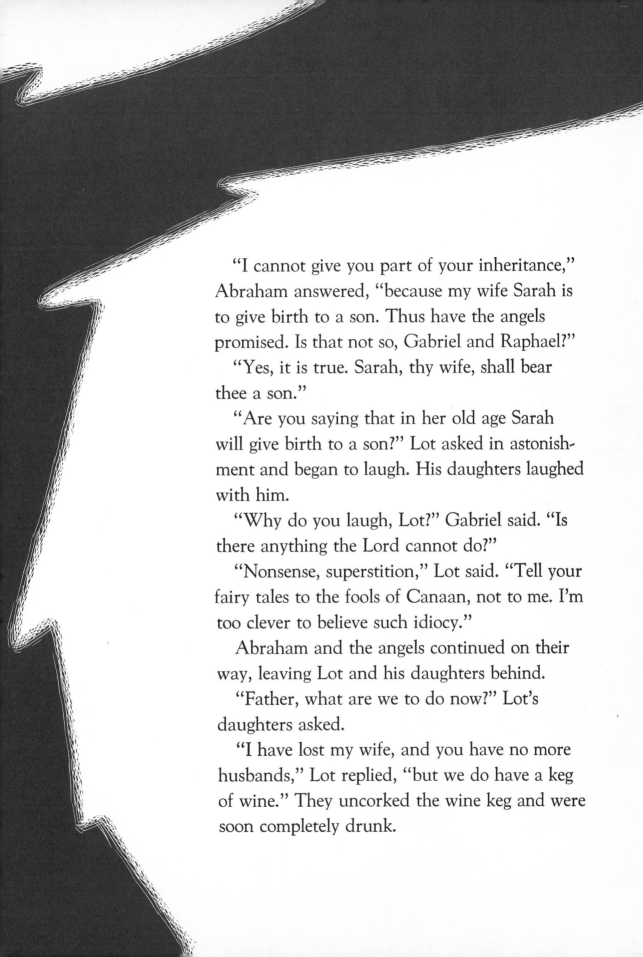

"I cannot give you part of your inheritance," Abraham answered, "because my wife Sarah is to give birth to a son. Thus have the angels promised. Is that not so, Gabriel and Raphael?"

"Yes, it is true. Sarah, thy wife, shall bear thee a son."

"Are you saying that in her old age Sarah will give birth to a son?" Lot asked in astonishment and began to laugh. His daughters laughed with him.

"Why do you laugh, Lot?" Gabriel said. "Is there anything the Lord cannot do?"

"Nonsense, superstition," Lot said. "Tell your fairy tales to the fools of Canaan, not to me. I'm too clever to believe such idiocy."

Abraham and the angels continued on their way, leaving Lot and his daughters behind.

"Father, what are we to do now?" Lot's daughters asked.

"I have lost my wife, and you have no more husbands," Lot replied, "but we do have a keg of wine." They uncorked the wine keg and were soon completely drunk.

After a while they found a cave, where they settled down and lived like savages. Except for defending criminals, there was nothing Lot knew how to do. His pampered daughters, who had learned little except how to eat, drink, and give orders to slaves and servants, and how to mock the poor, the beaten, and the sick, now lived in filth and sin.

The evil city of Sodom was never rebuilt. It remained a desert where not even wild animals ventured.

In time Lot again settled in some corrupt city and again became the champion of murderers, thieves, and swindlers. He never heard from Abraham again, but he no longer cared because he learned from wandering peddlers that the angels had spoken the truth; there would be no inheritance for him.

Abraham did not again visit his faithless nephew, Lot, and Lot's sinful daughters. Sarah bore Abraham a son just as the angels had predicted.

He was called Isaac. He, in turn, sired Jacob, from whom stem the Twelve Tribes of Israel.